EMERGENCY!

SMOKEJUMPERS

FIGHTING FIRES FROM THE SKY

by Justin Petersen

CAPSTONE PRESS
a capstone imprint

Edge Books are published by Capstone Press,
1710 Roe Crest Drive, North Mankato, Minnesota 56003
www.mycapstone.com

LIBRARY OF CONGRESS CATALOGING-IN-PUBLICATION DATA
Petersen, Justin, author.
Smokejumpers : fighting fires from the sky / by Justin Petersen.
pages cm.—(Edge books. Emergency)
Summary: "Gives readers a behind-the-scenes look at how emergency
responders do their day-to-day jobs"—Provided by publisher.
Audience: Ages 8-14.
Audience: Grades 4 to 6.
ISBN 978-1-4914-8030-4 (library binding)
ISBN 978-1-4914-8417-3 (ebook pdf)
1. Smokejumpers—Juvenile literature. 2. Smokejumping—Juvenile
literature. 3. Wildfire fighters—Juvenile literature. I. Title. II.
Title: Smoke jumpers.
SD421.23.P48 2016
634.9′618—dc23   2015034882

EDITORIAL CREDITS
Erin Butler, editor; Nicole Ramsay, designer; Sara Radka, media researcher

PHOTO CREDITS
freetextures: Texture18 cement, 2–32; Newscom.com: Darin Oswald/
MCT, cover, Chris Butler/ZUMA Press, 5, 7, 8, 9, 13, 17, 29, John Wagner/
ZUMApress, 11, David I. Gross/ZUMA Press, 14, Andreas Fuhrmann/ZUMA
Press, 19, Kim Ringeisen/Polaris, 21, NOAH BERGER/EPA, 22, H. Lorren Au
Jr/ZUMA Press, 23, Renee Jones Schneider/ZUMA Press, 25, Tim Wagner/
ZUMA Press, 27

Printed in the United States of America in Mankato, Minnesota.

TABLE OF CONTENTS

JUMPING INTO THE FIRE

Summer lightning strikes a tree in Fairbanks, Alaska. Smoke rolls across the sky as the tree begins to burn. The blaze could eat up 5,000 acres (2,023 hectares) of national forest in minutes if it is not contained. The local fire chief is concerned because his staff cannot contain the wildfire alone. The crew is too far away, and local firefighters do not carry the tools to contain a fire of this size. The fire chief has to call in the smokejumpers.

The best way for smokejumpers to get near the blaze is to use an **airdrop**. These specially trained firefighters parachute out of an airplane while carrying special tools to fight wildfires. They land close to the fire and contain it quickly. This is all in a day's work for smokejumpers, whose main job is to contain remote fires and swiftly relieve exhausted fire crews.

Since wildfires are common in the western United States, smokejumping has become a growing career. More than 300 smokejumpers work each year in the United States. The summer months are an extremely busy time for smokejumpers. On average, they make more than 1,200 jumps per year.

airdrop—delivery of cargo, emergency supplies, or people by parachute from an airplane in flight

Smokejumpers jump from aircraft as close to a wildfire as possible.

Chapter 1

BECOMING A SMOKEJUMPER

It's difficult to get hired as a smokejumper. Hiring organizations, called jump bases, require candidates to have basic firefighting skills and 12 months of experience in the field. People interested in becoming smokejumpers gain experience by training with units called hotshot crews or with local fire agencies. College education in forestry or agriculture is also helpful.

PHYSICAL FITNESS

Physical fitness is an important part of being a smokejumper. The training program begins with a fitness test called the physical training (PT) test. It takes place on the first day of **rookie** training. Candidates are tested in several activities. They begin by running 1.5 miles (2.4 kilometers) in 11 minutes. Then they must do seven pull-ups, 45 sit-ups, and 25 push-ups. If a candidate cannot complete these tasks, then he or she will not be accepted into training.

rookie—a person who has just started a job or activity and has little experience

suppression—an act or instance of putting down or holding back

Smokejumper rookies go through strenuous training to prepare them for firefighting.

FACT:
Hotshot crews consist of 20 firefighters specially trained in wildfire **suppression** tactics.

FACT:
Smokejumpers must learn how to tuck and roll when landing after the impact of a parachute jump. Since these firefighters carry such heavy gear, this important skill is essential for their own safety.

Field exercises are a safe way to practice the skills learned in training.

TRAINING

The training program to become a smokejumper lasts six weeks. It is designed for rookies to learn the basics of parachute jumping and handling tools on the ground. Training to become a smokejumper takes hard work. Trainees wake up at 5:00 a.m. and line up in formation to head out for a morning run. This warm-up run is just the beginning of a 12-hour day.

During an average day of training, rookie smokejumpers receive both physical and academic training. After their warm-up, they continue with more physical exercises. Then they enter the classroom to learn the basics of smokejumping. This includes skills such as parachuting and CPR. It also includes preparation and debriefing for field exercises.

The gear pack hike is the final training test. Candidates first strap on full gear packs weighing 115 pounds (52 kilograms). The packs include the tools and equipment needed to fight wildfires. Candidates must hike 3 miles (4.8 km) on level terrain in less than 90 minutes while carrying their packs.

In addition to field exercises, strengthening and cardiovascular exercises are a must to stay in good physical shape.

SKILLS AND FIELD EXERCISES

Smokejumpers learn many skills during training. Parachute jumping, using water pumps and chainsaws, tree climbing, and water landings are all required skills for smokejumpers. Parachute training and water landings help jumpers learn how to enter and exit dangerous situations. They are likely to face these kinds of situations while fighting wildfires in remote locations. Using chainsaws and climbing trees are skills that smokejumpers need to know to control fires. Chainsaws are used to cut down trees to create **firebreaks**. A well-trained smokejumper can identify which trees and structures to remove to slow down a fire's progress. Smokejumpers need to be able to climb trees in case any of their equipment gets stuck in a tree after their jump.

TECHNICAL EXERCISES

Orienteering and fire science are useful technical skills learned during training. Orienteering is the use of compasses and landmarks to **navigate** a region. The ability to locate and exit areas with wildfires could be the difference between life and death for a smokejumper. In addition, smokejumpers learn about how wildfires work on a scientific level. They use this information to help them stop fires from spreading.

firebreak—an area of land that has had plants and trees removed to stop the spread of a fire

navigate—to decide the direction a vehicle or person should travel

The First Jump

A smokejumper's first jump is a team effort and an unforgettable experience, but many veteran smokejumpers say that the first jump isn't scary. Rookies are often more concerned with correctly performing their duties on the ground than with jumping out of a plane. Spotters provide rookie smokejumpers with radios on their first jump. They then talk the trainees down during their descent from the plane. Michael Blinn described his first jump as something he'd remember forever: "As I exited the door, I watched my feet rise toward the horizon and felt the snap of the parachute deploying. The sudden total silence and extreme clarity of the canopy against blue sky above me was an unparalleled experience. I'll never forget it."

Smokejumpers practice jumps in many different conditions and terrains.

FACT:
Only four smokejumpers have died during a parachute jump since 1940.

Chapter 2

PREPARATION AND EQUIPMENT

Smokejumpers rely on gear that can be dropped with them by airplane. The gear helps **extinguish** the fires and keeps them safe. Parachutes and protective clothes are their most important supplies.

Padded clothes protect smokejumpers during a parachute landing, including landing among trees and on the ground. The padded clothing also helps protect smokejumpers from the fire itself. Smokejumper suits are made of a protective material called Kevlar. Kevlar is thick, durable, and fire resistant. The suits are designed to protect smokejumpers from fire. One padded suit can weigh up to 75 pounds (34 kg).

Smokejumpers operate two types of parachutes, depending on the hiring organization. The Forest Service provides round parachutes, while the Bureau of Land Management uses ram air sports parachutes. Parachutes allow smokejumpers to reach the best strategic area to fight the fire.

extinguish—to cause something to stop burning

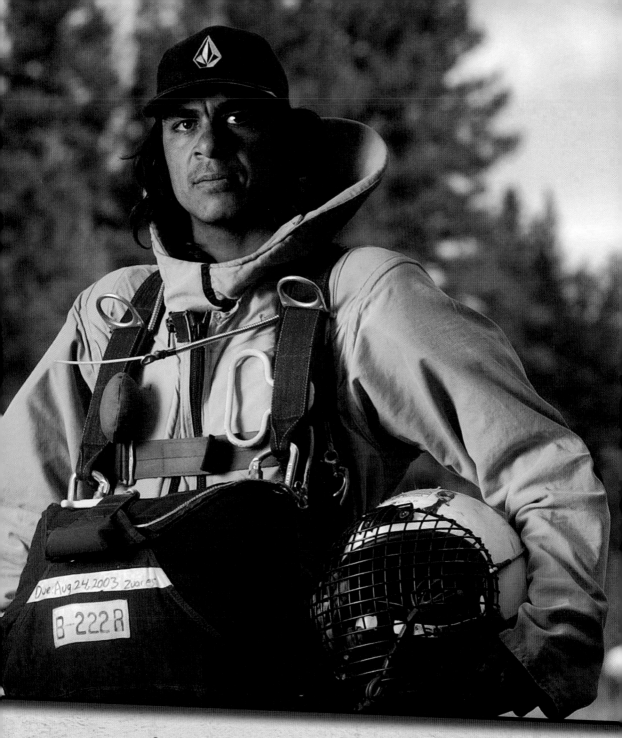

Smokejumpers wear protective gear and carry firefighting tools.

Firefighters use pulaskis to clear areas around spot fires.

Chainsaws are used to cut firelines and clear paths for other firefighters.

TOOLS

Fireboxes are kits filled with tools and supplies for smokejumper crews. They typically last for three days, with enough supplies for two people. An airplane drops more supplies if they run out. The firebox contains everything necessary to fight fires, as well as food and water. Even chainsaws are packed safely in the firebox.

In addition to chainsaws, smokejumpers use a special ax called the **pulaski**. The tool combines an ax and **adze** in one head. It can be used to both dig soil and chop wood. The McLeod is another useful device in the field. It is a two-sided blade with a long handle like a rake. This tool is designed to rake firebreaks with one side and to cut trees with the other. Smokejumpers also use crosscut saws that are operated by two team members. Crosscut saws are less susceptible to damage than chainsaws when dropped from the plane.

Portable water pumps are required on fire missions in wilderness areas. They are also dropped in the firebox. The water pumps help transport water and firefighting chemicals that cannot be used, like a water system within city limits.

pulaski–firefighting tool that is a combination ax and digging tool

adze–a cutting tool that has a thin curved blade and that is usually used for shaping wood

TRAVELING TO THE SCENE

Planes used by smokejumpers must be able to safely deliver a crew to the site of a wildfire. These planes travel less than 300 miles (483 km) per trip. Some smokejumper planes include **turbine** engine DC-3s, Twin Otters, Dornier, Casa, and Shorts Serpas. They are designed to carry up to 20 firefighters at a time.

Pilots say that fires create their own weather. Wildfires can cause gusty winds, and the smoky conditions they generate can affect air travel. Pilots for smokejumper planes need to take this into account when flying.

CREWS

Smokejumper teams vary in size from two to 20 people. Every team has a spotter, who flies with the team. The spotter is an experienced smokejumper who functions as the mission leader on air operations. He evaluates wind and other factors to determine if the jump is possible.

Additional jumper roles include type III incident commanders, division supervisors, strike team leaders, and air tactical group supervisors on fire assignments. Though many of these are leadership roles, everyone on the team ends up working together to fight the fire.

turbine—an engine powered by steam or gas; the steam or gas moves through the blades of a fanlike device and makes it turn

Smokejumper planes are specially outfitted to carry firefighters and their gear.

THE JUMP

When the siren sounds signaling a fire, the smokejumper team springs into action right away. Since their fireboxes are always ready to go, smokejumpers pack the supplies into the plane, strap on their smokejumper suits, and grab their parachutes. Once they are in the plane, they receive more details about the fire, including its location and size.

The team's spotter watches from the window for the best place to jump to fight the fire. This requires good orienteering skills and knowledge of fire science. Once the most strategic point is located, the crewmembers make the jump. They land by tucking and rolling their bodies to avoid injury.

Once they are on the ground, the team sets up camp. Team members must be prepared to spend days at a time fighting fires in the wilderness. Fireboxes contain necessary supplies for survival. The smokejumpers carry sleeping bags and other supplies themselves by attaching them to their uniforms.

Smokejumpers must carefully aim their landings for their safety.

forester–a person who takes care of forests by planting trees, cutting down trees, and completing other forestry duties

Why do smokejumpers jump?

The idea for firefighters to parachute into a wildfire first arose in 1934. A man working as a **forester** named T.V. Pearson came up with the idea. He reasoned that firefighters could use parachutes to get right to the best spot for fighting a fire. That way, they would not already be worn out by the time they began their work. Thanks to Pearson's idea, the first fire jump

Chapter 3

CHALLENGES OF SMOKEJUMPING

One summer day, a forest fire starts when lightning strikes in a dry, heavily wooded area. A call comes into the jump base, and the crew leaps into action.

While the pilot ferries the plane from the hangar, three smokejumpers prepare two fireboxes and check their gear. The team loads up, takes off, and heads north. Within 15 minutes, they are ready to jump. The fire has covered 30 acres (12.1 hectares), and the wind is picking up.

The first smokejumper glances down at the burning grass and trees 10,000 feet (3,048 meters) below the airplane. He checks to make sure the pressure gauge is working. The pressure gauge helps to monitor speed during the jump. Next, he throws a blue paper streamer from the plane. It glides west of the fire, indicating the direction of the wind. The smokejumper steps out of the plane, still watching the streamer, and his two partners follow.

The three land on a rocky hillside, tucking and rolling as they were trained to do. After setting up camp, they decide who will use which tool, and they start working. The wind finally dies down, and the fire is contained in two days. But before leaving, the group must make sure that the fire is completely cool. By the fifth day, the ground is cool, and the crew is picked up safely.

Navigating to and around wildfires can be dangerous and must be done with caution.

Firefighters discuss plans while fighting a 2015 fire near Clearlake, California.

FACT:
Russia employs the most smokejumpers of any country in the world.

RISKS FOR SMOKEJUMPERS

During a smokejumper's risky mission, there are many things that can go wrong. Nature and unpredictable circumstances can be dangerous. No firefighting scenario is the same, and sometimes things do not go according to plan.

Strong winds can fuel a wildfire. If the wind picks up, it can feed the fire and make it grow faster. It can also blow the fire in a different direction than a smokejumper unit plans. If a fire unit's position is overcome by fire, it can lead to serious injury or death. Compromised supplies can also affect the outcome of a mission. For example, if a water pump is punctured on the drop, it cannot be used in a timely fashion, or possibly at all.

One unexpected turn came during the Yarnell Hill Fire in Arizona. This fire overran and killed 19 members of the Granite Mountain Hotshots on June 30, 2013. The catastrophe was a result of winds that reached 22 miles (35 kilometers) per hour. Only one member of the team, Brendan McDonough, survived. He had been serving as the lookout.

Firefighters use personal fire shelters in the event that there is no escape from a raging wildfire.

INJURIES

Smokejumpers can also run into trouble before reaching the fire. In one case, a smokejumper named Erinkate Springer was injured on a parachute drop in Montana. She tore a ligament called an **ACL** when she landed, an injury that threatened her career as a smokejumper. In another case, a smokejumper named Lester Lycklama was using a **crosscut saw** to cut down a tree near a wildfire in Idaho. A section of the tree snapped off and struck Lycklama, killing him. These kinds of accidents are not uncommon. The combination of the wilderness and intense physical activity makes smokejumping risky. Even if an accident does not cause death or serious injury, it can set back the firefighting mission.

Trees are cut down in burned areas to keep them from falling on firefighters.

ACL–anterior cruciate ligament; a ligament of each knee that attaches the front of the tibia with the back of the femur

crosscut saw–a saw designed chiefly to cut across the grain of wood

Mann Gulch Fire

In August 1949, smokejumpers were called to Helena National Forest in Montana to fight what became known as the Mann Gulch Fire. A team of 15 smokejumpers assisted with a fire at the nearby campground. A sudden change in wind direction created a deadly scenario where the fire burned back uphill. It covered 3,000 acres (1,214 hectares) in only 10 minutes. The fire claimed the lives of 12 smokejumpers. This was in spite of efforts by R. Wagner "Wag" Dodge, the smokejumpers' foreman, to implement emergency safety procedures. It took five days to contain the massive blaze. The disaster led the U.S. government to create new training procedures and protocols for smokejumping.

Chapter 4

SMOKEJUMPERS IN EVERYDAY LIFE

Smokejumpers leave camp when fire season has passed. They return before the next season for a two-week refresher course. The course includes preparing with practice jumps. The goal is to perform 15 practice jumps before dropping into a live-fire scenario.

Physical training is such an important aspect of the job that many smokejumpers make sure to exercise, including running and doing push-ups, every day. It is important for a smokejumper to show up in shape for fire season.

Even during the fire season, smokejumpers may not fight fires every day. When there is no wildfire call, smokejumpers spend their time manufacturing and repairing equipment. They work to make sure that they are always ready at a moment's notice to jump into a plane and fight a fire.

Smokejumpers must ensure that their equipment is in good repair at all times.

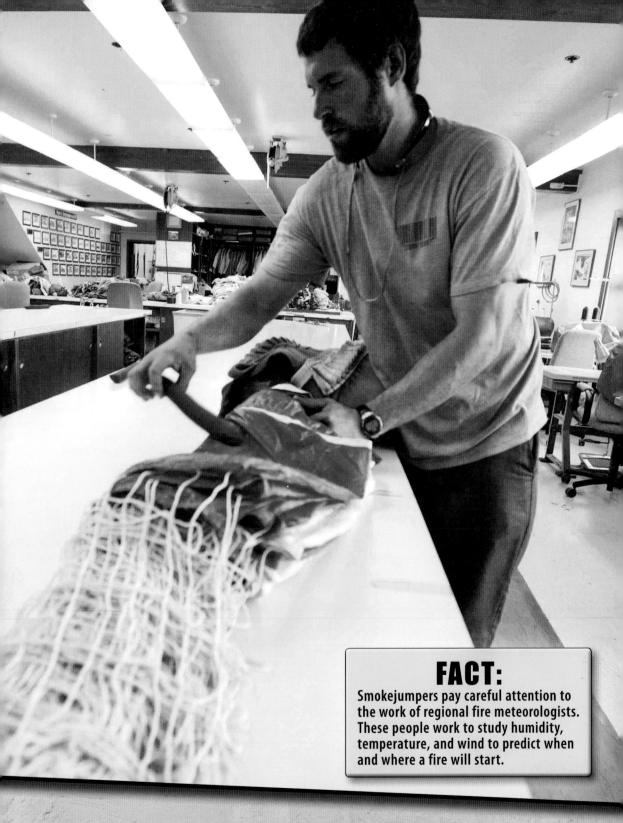

The goal of a smokejumper is to protect natural resources, homes, and businesses that are threatened by forest fires. Each smokejumper's role is essential in containing fires in remote locations that local firefighters cannot reach. Planes and orienteering allow smokejumpers to reach these remote locations. Smokejumper training is specialized and unique, including parachute diving and even tree climbing. Once they are trained, smokejumpers brave the challenge of jumping out of an airplane and camping out in the wilderness to fight fire.

Smokejumpers dedicate large amounts of their time and resources to difficult training. After training, they risk their safety and even their lives every fire season. Thanks to smokejumpers, people and nature are safer from the threat of wildfires.

Smokejumpers are respected for their dedication and bravery by fellow firefighters and civilians alike.

FACT:
The United States employs more than 270 smokejumpers.

Firefighting Elite

Jason Ramos has fought fires for 25 years, first as an urban firefighter and now as a smokejumper in Winthrop, Okanogan County, in Washington State. Ramos knows that becoming a smokejumper is no easy job. Applicants need to have years of experience and try out before they are even considered. Still, Ramos thinks it is worth it. He says, "With any fire agency, when you come in, you're going to hear about all the different job opportunities. Smokejumping was always at the top." Smokejumpers are highly respected by

GLOSSARY

ACL (ay-see-EHL)—anterior cruciate ligament; a ligament of each knee that attaches the front of the tibia with the back of the femur

adze (ADZ)—a cutting tool that has a thin curved blade and that is usually used for shaping wood

airdrop (AYR-drahp)—delivery of cargo, emergency supplies, or people by parachute from an airplane in flight

crosscut saw (KRAWS-khut SAH)—a saw designed chiefly to cut across the grain of wood

extinguish (ik-STING-gwish)—to cause something to stop burning

firebreak (FYR-brayk)—an area of land that has had plants and trees removed to stop the spread of a fire

forester (FOR-ih-stuhr)—a person who takes care of forests by planting trees, cutting down trees, and completing other forestry duties

navigate (NAV-uh-gate)—to decide the direction a vehicle or person should travel

pulaski (pul-ASS-kee)—firefighting tool that is a combination ax and digging tool

rookie (RUK-ee)—a person who has just started a job or activity and has little experience

suppression (suh-PREH-shuhn)—an act or instance of putting down or holding back

turbine (TUR-bine)—an engine powered by steam or gas; the steam or gas moves through the blades of a fanlike device and makes it turn

READ MORE

Goldish, Meish. *Smokejumpers.* New York: Bearport Publishing, 2014.

Gordon, Nick. *Smoke Jumper.* Dangerous Jobs. Minneapolis: Torque Books, 2012.

Mara, Will. *Smokejumper.* North Mankato, Minn.: Cherry Lake Publishing, 2015.

Tieck, Sarah. *Smoke Jumpers.* Edina, Minn.: Abdo Publishing Company, 2011.

CRITICAL THINKING USING THE COMMON CORE

1. How are smokejumpers different from average firefighters? What kind of fires do they fight? (Key Ideas and Details)

2. What are some pieces of equipment smokejumpers use? How does this equipment help them fight fires? (Key Ideas and Details)

3. How do you think practice jumps and exercises differ from real emergencies? (Integration of Knowledge and Ideas)

INTERNET SITES

FactHound offers a safe, fun way to find Internet sites related to this book. All of the sites on FactHound have been researched by our staff.

Here's all you do:

Visit *www.facthound.com*

Type in this code: 9781491480304

INDEX